CVJC

Happy Holidays!

Hanukkah

by Rebecca Sabelko

BELLWETHER MEDIA
MINNEAPOLIS, MN

Blastoff! Beginners are developed by literacy experts and educators to meet the needs of early readers. These engaging informational texts support young children as they begin reading about their world. Through simple language and high frequency words paired with crisp, colorful photos, Blastoff! Beginners launch young readers into the universe of independent reading.

Blastoff! Universe

Reading Level — Grade K

Grades 1-3

Grade 4

Sight Words in This Book 🔍

a	get	of	the
day	in	oil	they
each	is	one	to
eat	it	people	with
for	new	play	

This edition first published in 2023 by Bellwether Media, Inc.

No part of this publication may be reproduced in whole or in part without written permission of the publisher. For information regarding permission, write to Bellwether Media, Inc., Attention: Permissions Department, 6012 Blue Circle Drive, Minnetonka, MN 55343.

Library of Congress Cataloging-in-Publication Data

LC record for Hanukkah available at: https://lccn.loc.gov/2022009294

Text copyright © 2023 by Bellwether Media, Inc. BLASTOFF! BEGINNERS and associated logos are trademarks and/or registered trademarks of Bellwether Media, Inc.

Editor: Christina Leaf   Designer: Laura Sowers

Printed in the United States of America, North Mankato, MN.

Table of Contents

It Is Hanukkah!

It is the
Festival of Lights!
Happy Hanukkah!

When Is Hanukkah?

It is in November or December. It lasts eight nights and days.

It is a
Jewish holiday.

It honors
a **miracle**!
Oil for light
lasted eight days.

Eight Special Nights!

Families light **menorahs.** They light a new candle each night.

menorah

People give
thanks to God.
They sing.

Kids play with a *dreidel*.
It spins.
They get prizes!

dreidel

People give gifts.
Kids get one
each day.

Families eat foods fried in oil.
They remember the past!

fried food

Hanukkah Facts

Celebrating Hanukkah

dreidel

menorah

gifts

Hanukkah Activities

light
menorah

play with
dreidel

give gifts

Glossary

festival

a joyful event or holiday

Jewish

related to a religion with one God that began in Israel

menorahs

candle holders

miracle

an event often believed to be from God

To Learn More

ON THE WEB

FACTSURFER

Factsurfer.com gives you a safe, fun way to find more information.

1. Go to www.factsurfer.com.

2. Enter "Hanukkah" into the search box and click 🔍.

3. Select your book cover to see a list of related content.

Index

The images in this book are reproduced through the courtesy of: Maglara, front cover; Lisa F. Young, p. 3; FamVeld, pp. 4-5; Drazen Zigic, pp. 6-7, 8-9, 23 (festival, miracle); Golden Pixels LLC, pp. 10-11; Africa Studio, pp. 12, 22 (light menorah); Noam Armonn, pp. 12-13; ASAP/ Alamy, pp. 14-15; Moti Meiri, p. 16; kali9, pp. 16-17, 22 (play with dreidel); The Good Brigade/ Getty, pp. 18-19; Food Impressions, p. 20; ChameleonsEye, pp. 20-21; tomertu, p. 22; Pixel-Shot, p. 22 (give gifts); photoshooter2015, p. 23 (Jewish); New Africa, p. 23 (menorahs).